Conversations With My Soul
An Authentic Journaling Guide

Companion to the Workbook
Creative Healing Through Transformation

Donna Fitzgerald & Tana Heminsley

CONVERSATIONS WITH MY SOUL

AN AUTHENTIC JOURNALING GUIDE

Donna Fitzgerald

&

Tana Heminsley

 Daring to Share Global

Published by Donna Fitzgerald and Tana Heminsley
November 2021 ISBN: 9781777549510

Copyright © 2021 by Donna Fitzgerald and Tana Heminsley All rights reserved. No part of this publication may be reproduced, stored in or introduced into a retrieval system, or transmitted, in any form, or by any means (electronic, mechanical, photocopying, recording or otherwise) without the prior written permission of the publisher. This book is sold subject to the condition that it shall not, by way of trade or otherwise, be lent, resold, hired out, or otherwise circulated without the publisher's prior consent in any form of binding or cover other than that in which it is published and without a similar condition including this condition being imposed on the subsequent purchaser.

Editor: Diana Reyers
Typeset: Greg Salisbury
Book Cover Design: Olli Vidal

DISCLAIMER: Readers of this publication agree that, neither Donna Fitzgerald, Tana Heminsley, or Daring to Share Global will be held responsible or liable for damages that may be alleged as resulting directly or indirectly from the use of this publication. Neither the lead publisher nor the self-publishing author can be held accountable for the information provided by, or actions, resulting from, accessing these resources

By Tana Heminsley

EASE Amidst Challenging Times:
Simple Practices For Inner Peace Beyond COVID

Awaken Your Authentic Leadership:
Authentic Leadership Conversations
for Meaningful Connection

Awaken Your Authentic Leadership:
Lead with Inner Clarity and Purpose
Awaken Your Authentic Leadership: Authenticity Journal

Daring to Share:
There to Here - 2nd Edition | Volume 1
Tana Heminsley, Contributing Author

Daring to Share:
8 Brave Souls Sharing Their Authentic Road Trip—Volume 1
Tana Heminsley, Contributing Author

By Donna Fitzgerald

Creative Healing Through Transformation:
Conversations with My Soul
Workbook
Donna Fitzgerald, Co-Author
Tana Heminsley, Co-Author

Daring to Share:
There to Here - 2nd Edition | Volume 1
Donna Fitzgerald, Contributing Author

Daring to Share:
8 Brave Souls Sharing Their Authentic Road Trip—Volume 1
Donna Fitzgerald, Contributing Author

TESTIMONIALS

I applaud the authors for this beautiful healing book that could only have been written by someone who has successfully navigated the lived experience of major loss and change in life direction. The frameworks and exercises in this book provide really practical stepping stones for the reader through this difficult and uncharted territory – a route that enables the reader to realize the power of emotional intelligence, spirituality and authenticity to successfully transcend the most profoundly difficult life experiences. I urge anyone who has suffered such a life changing loss to use this highly empowering and insightful guide to navigate towards a place of healing for the mind and soul.

Mike Fitzpatrick,
Physician and Chief of Staff, KHSC
Kingston, Ontario, Canada

I am honoured to be asked to write a few words about this workbook, Creative Healing Through Transformation, written by Donna Fitzgerald. I am a Rehabilitation Physician and have spent my career working with individuals and caregivers affected by ALS and other neuromuscular conditions. I witnessed Donna's personal journey through the many stages of providing care for a loved one while still balancing many other roles. All of us in the Neuromuscular Clinic witnessed her adjustment and recovery and we were pleased that she continued to work through the ALS Society as a peer support for other caregivers. Peer support is such a critical part of the supports offered to individuals. Peers bring the lived experience and validation of the broad breath of emotion that caregivers may feel. I am pleased that Donna has written this workbook so that she and others can continue to help caregivers. The workbook shares her personal stories in a way that encourages other to follow the path of healing. It is a wonderfully guided journey, while not being prescriptive, that can be used by individuals, in support networks and with peer support. Thank you, Donna, for writing and sharing this, I am confident that it will help others.

Karen M. Smith MD
Kingston, Ontario, Canada

Rich Resource Guide. In this rich resource guide, the author provides a practical step by step approach to self-discovery through journaling. With empathy and compassion, she walks alongside the reader, acknowledging the fear and anxiety that may accompany such an introspective journey. She encourages and supports the reader throughout the process, providing useful tips and guidance along the way. By sharing frank and honest insights into her personal story of loss, followed by her journey of self-discovery, self-awareness and renewal, the author provides a unique and authentic voice to the power of journaling. The result is a practical and welcome addition to the toolbox of resources for caregivers across a wide spectrum.

Patti Dixon-Medora,
Caregiver Support Group Facilitator,
Alzheimer Society of KFL&A,
Kingston, Ontario, Canada

This is an amazing workbook. Well written and simple to follow. The author shows, through personal anecdotes, a courageous journey that will aid others to also take the steps necessary for personal growth. Whether experiencing personal loss and grief or wanting to lead a more authentic and emotionally healthy life, this workbook provides the reader with excellent examples and exercises that can help lead to a richer understanding of ones' Self.

Sylvia Simonyi-Elmer, B.Sc, DCS, RP
Registered Psychotherapist
Kingston, Ontario, Canada

If you are looking for a structured way to help you on your journey to improved self-awareness and the peace that comes with living an authentic life, then this book is for you. Donna and Tana's handbook provides clear and compassionate tools for caregivers to help them re-discover who they are in the face of their role as a caregiver. Each chapter offers descriptions and activities that can be easily incorporated into a caregiver's daily routine. And the pay-off is tremendous – discovering self-awareness; finding your true inner voice and living an authentic life. Donna's honest and, at times, vulnerable journaling is both helpful and uplifting as an example of how using these tools can help a caregiver grow to become the person they are meant to be.

Teresa Whalen
Kingston, Ontario, Canada

Journaling Steps

Journaling Step 1: Creating Self-Awareness 1
Journaling Step 2: Experiencing Emotional Feelings 9
Journaling Step 3: Discovering Your Values 17
Journaling Step 4: Clarifying Your Inner Purpose Feeling 25
Journaling Step 5: Managing Your Inner Critic 33
Journaling Step 6: Finding Inner Balance 41
Journaling Step 7: Setting Personal Boundaries 49
Journaling Step 8, Part 1: Navigating Transitions 57
Journaling Step 8, Part 2: Envisioning the Future 65

INTRODUCTION
BY DONNA FITZGERALD

This journal you hold in your hands is your first step to rediscovering the beautiful soul you are. I am proud to offer this companion journal to the Creative Healing Through Transformation: Conversations with My Soul workbook. Introducing this valuable tool into your self-care routine can also be the starting point in learning to express yourself without the workbook. My hope is that you start your practice and look forward to this daily sacred time with your soul. I have journaled every day for twenty years, and my practice evolved and transitioned into me now enjoying free-flow writing.

To get started, find a quiet, comfortable spot in your home that speaks to you. Pick a time of the day when you won't be disturbed. You may choose to start a half-hour earlier than your day normally begins. It can be helpful to take a few deep cleansing breaths to settle your body into this new activity. You may experience some resistance if you've been on full-speed autopilot up until now.

In the beginning, set a timer for ten minutes and write what first comes to mind. The words and phrases don't need to connect. You will simply be emptying what is within your conscious mind. With time and practice, you will be able to sit and be in the moment, releasing your thoughts freely. Be gentle with the process and be aware that there may be emotions you have been pushing down that come to the surface. Allow them to move through you.

My passion in life has been to support caregivers and those feeling lost, alone, and disconnected from themselves. This can happen so gradually through the caregiving role that you don't even realize you are losing parts of yourself until an event or moment within your chaotic life jolts you into awareness.

My vision for this journal is a tool to use through all stages of your caregiver journey. You may be at the beginning of your caregiver role, you may be deep in the depths of the chaos and demands of caregiving, or you may have just completed your journey with your loved one and are now faced with working through grief and creating a new life. Wherever you find yourself on your personal journey is the best place to start. There are so many demands in your life, and unfortunately, you may have forgotten to put yourself on the list of receiving care. Today is a good day to start.

I was a caregiver for my late husband from 1998 to 2004. After four years in that role, I found myself experiencing caregiver burnout. I had lost who I was. It was a terrifying place to be, and I made a commitment to myself to find my way back. Journaling was a gift I gave myself to support my healing through caregiving, grief, loss, and moving forward in my new life.

Unfortunately, as a caregiver, I felt I was not always seen. No one sat down with me at the beginning of that role to explain what a beautiful gift I was giving my husband and the amount of energy it would take. Nor did they explain the importance of creating pockets of time for my self-care. I know I would have been able to cope longer if I had started self-care practices earlier.

If I had known the importance of the gifts of engaging in free-flow activities like practicing journaling, getting out into nature, and having weekly dates with myself, I would have scheduled more time for them without feeling guilty. I eventually learned that if I was not healthy emotionally, physically, and spiritually, I could not sustain supporting my husband, my family or myself. Journaling helped me process all the emotions that come with the ever-changing caregiving role, the grieving process, and the transition into a new chapter of life.

Creating Self-Awareness

Journaling Step 1

How can being self-aware support you on your path to self-discovery?

**Excerpt From
Creative Healing Through Transformation:
Conversations With My Soul**

I was introduced to journaling twenty years ago while struggling with the demands of caring for my husband with Lou Gehrig's disease, otherwise known as ALS, working full-time, and raising my family.
I started therapy to help navigate the emotions, fears, and thoughts that became part of my life.
The therapist suggested journaling, and I discovered that writing was the greatest gift I gave myself twenty years ago, providing me with the ability to maintain a conversation with my soul, my inner voice, every day.

~ Donna Fitzgerald

An Authentic Journaling Guide

Journaling Step 1

An Authentic Journaling Guide

Journaling Step 1

An Authentic Journaling Guide

Journaling Step 1

An Authentic Journaling Guide

Experiencing Emotional Feelings

Journaling Step 2

What emotions are you experiencing at this time in your life?

**Excerpt From
Creative Healing Through Transformation:
Conversations With My Soul**

A year after my husband died, I remember
focusing on experiencing my emotions.
I was spending a lot of time journaling and working
through the grieving process.
What was revealed was that I was still healing and had not
introduced people into my life or thought about
the future for a very long time.
A year later, I consciously reflected about my emotions again,
but this time it was very different because my journaling
allowed me to open up to new awareness and self-discovery.

~ Donna Fitzgerald

An Authentic Journaling Guide

Journaling Step 2

An Authentic Journaling Guide

Journaling Step 2

An Authentic Journaling Guide

Journaling Step 2

An Authentic Journaling Guide

Discovering Your Values

Journaling Step 3

How can your values support you to develop more awareness about yourself while caregiving on your self-discovery path?

Excerpt From
Creative Healing Through Transformation:
Conversations With My Soul

I reflect on my value of Community Service, if all is aligned, the emotion I feel is meaningful. When I am true to myself within my service to others, whether it be volunteering, helping clients on their path to self-discovery, or supporting individuals in my community, I am aware of how in line I am with my Community Service value because I feel meaningful when supporting others.

~ Donna Fitzgerald

An Authentic Journaling Guide

Journaling Step 3

An Authentic Journaling Guide

Journaling Step 3

An Authentic Journaling Guide

Journaling Step 3

An Authentic Journaling Guide

Clarifying My Inner Purpose Feeling

Journaling Step 4

How can being aware of your Inner Purpose Feeling support you to connect with your soul within the journey of caregiving?

Excerpt From
Creative Healing Through Transformation:
Conversations With My Soul

My Inner Purpose Feeling is Calm, and my Enneagram personality is the Peacemaker, and I want to help everyone. When I feel balanced within my everyday life, I feel a sense of calm; when I don't, I feel anxious within every aspect of my being, life, and supportive role. When I was a caregiver for my husband for six years, working full-time, raising our family, providing emotional support and nursing care to my husband, I tried to keep our home life as normal as possible. Unfortunately, I forgot that I, too, needed to be on the list of care.

~ Donna Fitzgerald

An Authentic Journaling Guide

Journaling Step 4

An Authentic Journaling Guide

Journaling Step 4

An Authentic Journaling Guide

Journaling Step 4

An Authentic Journaling Guide

Managing Your Inner Critic

Journaling Step 5

How can you use your inner critic to determine what you believe and feel while caregiving and discovering more about yourself?

Excerpt From
Creative Healing Through Transformation:
Conversations With My Soul

I can determine when my inner critic speaks from a past pattern or thought, and I have become more authentic and in tune with my inner voice—my soul.
My inner critic has become a welcomed part of my being. I now have the confidence to really evaluate my thoughts and connect with my values and Inner Purpose Feeling and receive the true message my inner critic is telling me. Maybe it is something I still need to heal, or a warning to be careful, or merely a thought I can let go of.

~ Donna Fitzgerald

An Authentic Journaling Guide

_____
_____
_____
_____
_____
_____
_____
_____
_____
_____
_____
_____
_____
_____
_____
_____
_____
_____
_____
_____
_____

Journaling Step 5

An Authentic Journaling Guide

Journaling Step 5

An Authentic Journaling Guide

Journaling Step 5

An Authentic Journaling Guide

Finding Inner Balance

Journaling Step 6

How can you consciously create inner balance to inspire journaling and self-discovery?

Excerpt From
Creative Healing Through Transformation:
Conversations With My Soul

I am at my best when I am calm and peaceful within myself.
I need structure and know what needs to be done to keep everyone in my life happy and healthy. As I follow my self-care routine, I feel energized and have the focus and drive to meet daily tasks.
I don't require much contact with others as I find being in the presence of too many people drains my energy.
I set healthy boundaries to help me manage my daily living.

~ Donna Fitzgerald

An Authentic Journaling Guide

Journaling Step 6

An Authentic Journaling Guide

Journaling Step 6

An Authentic Journaling Guide

Journaling Step 6

An Authentic Journaling Guide

Setting Personal Boundaries

Journaling Step 7

How can you create boundaries to support self-care while caregiving?

Excerpt From
Creative Healing Through Transformation:
Conversations With My Soul

As a caregiver, you have chosen to support and advocate for your loved one while they progress through their illness. You give your unconditional love to care for them; a role I would do again in a heartbeat.
What I would do differently is set personal boundaries earlier in my caregiver role.
Through my journey, I learned to meet my needs while giving to those I love—understanding the importance of my emotional and physical health contributed positively to the care of my loved one. I also learned that the progression of a disease and the circumstances surrounding it are out of my control. However, what I do have control over is how I connect with myself to reach the demands of everyday life in a more authentic way.

~ Donna Fitzgerald

An Authentic Journaling Guide

Journaling Step 7

An Authentic Journaling Guide

Journaling Step 7

An Authentic Journaling Guide

Journaling Step 7

An Authentic Journaling Guide

Navigating Transitions

Journaling Step 8
Part 1

How can you move through caregiving while creating new awareness moving towards the future?

**Excerpt From
Creative Healing Through Transformation:
Conversations With My Soul**

Transitions take time and require patience in order to listen to the conversations your soul so desperately wants you to pay attention to. Developing self-awareness of your patterns around patience and impatience and developing compassion for yourself, can be helpful. Being open to what feels right takes you in an entirely different direction than when you try to force a way of being.

~ Donna Fitzgerald

An Authentic Journaling Guide

Journaling Step 8 - Part 1

An Authentic Journaling Guide

Journaling Step 8 - Part 1

An Authentic Journaling Guide

Journaling Step 8 - Part 1

An Authentic Journaling Guide

Envisioning The Future

Journaling Step 8
Part 2

How can you create a vision for your life after caregiving?

**Excerpt From
Creative Healing Through Transformation:
Conversations With My Soul**

Visioning through journaling will reveal what you feel subconsciously and may not be aware of. Along with your newfound daily practice of self-discovery through journaling, you have likely begun to notice more clarity about what your authentic future looks and feels like.
Continuing on this path, you will also discover that you can better articulate your new path of personal transformation. Journaling will naturally reveal your vision without you realizing it is happening.

~ Donna Fitzgerald

An Authentic Journaling Guide

_____
_____
_____
_____
_____
_____
_____
_____
_____
_____
_____
_____
_____
_____
_____
_____
_____
_____
_____
_____
_____
_____
_____
_____

Journaling Step 8 - Part 2

An Authentic Journaling Guide

Journaling Step 8 - Part 2

An Authentic Journaling Guide

Journaling Step 8 - Part 2

An Authentic Journaling Guide

Climbing the Mountain
By Donna Fitzgerald

I lived happily at the bottom of the mountain for most of my life. I created a life with marriage and family in the forefront, and everything else came behind my true joy. In an instant, there was a mountain placed in my path. My husband's diagnosis of ALS now blocked the path. Could I go around it? Could I go over it? I started the path up the mountain—a journey I wasn't prepared for with the weight of my responsibilities. This included endless hours of walking that path, day and night, with difficulty breathing thinner air.

I had a choice. I could turn around and go back down the mountain and remain there in the valley that held my family in the life we had and remain living in the past. Or I could continue up the mountain and be awakened to the courage and strength that lay dormant inside me, providing me with the opportunity to test myself.

I stumbled and fell backwards, feeling defeated but knew I could not stay there. I had to trudge onward and upward. It was a journey I had to make on my own through the chill of the rain and the emptiness I felt. I decided to put one foot in front of the other.

The higher up the mountain, I discovered the awakening to the beauty of the life in front of me. There were blue skies and fluffy white clouds, and I adapted to the thin air. My body became stronger and my mind clearer as I spent all this time with myself.

I could see the top of the mountain and was no longer afraid of what was ahead of me because I conquered every challenge journeying forward and stood victorious on the top of the mountain. I shouted at the top of my lungs: Thank You!

I did not do this alone! I found my voice, confidence, passion, and purpose on the journey.

And as I made my way back down the mountain, I brought along the strength and knowing that I am alive, and by living every day with a sense of gratitude and wonder, I will never waste a day.

The trip down the other side continues to be done with joy, ease, and possibilities.

When met with a new challenge, I think of the mountain I already climbed and take strength from that journey.

ABOUT TANA HEMINSLEY

Tana is an Author, the Founder of Authentic Leadership Global™ as well as a retired, award-winning Leadership Coach.

She was awarded the *Vancouver Charter Chapter of the International Coach Federation's 2016 Coach Impact Award*. In 2019 she received the *CEO Magazine's Business Consultant Award* and was a *Book Excellence Awards Finalist* for her second book - *Awaken Your Authentic Leadership - Authenticity Journal*.

Tana has published three books in the *Awaken Your Authentic Leadership* series - about how to be your best self as an organizational leader. She has also written her first book for a broader audience titled *EASE Amidst Challenging Times: Simple Practices for Inner Peace Beyond COVID*.

She has spoken to audiences at hundreds of engagements and was a keynote speaker at the 2018 China Executive and Leadership Coaching Summit in Beijing.

Tana has more than 35 years of business and leadership experience, is a thought-leader in the area of Authentic Leadership and Emotional Intelligence and has been researching and practicing mindfulness for more than 15 years.

Tana lives in beautiful British Columbia, BC Canada, with her husband, Chris and cat, Buddy.

ABOUT
DONNA FITZGERALD

Donna is a Facilitator of Authentic Leadership Conversations,™ co-author of Daring to Share There to Here, Volume 1 by Diana Reyers, and an active member of the Daring to Share Global,™ team.

She volunteered with the Kingston Chapter of the ALS Society in Kingston, Ontario, Canada for eight years, providing support to families living with ALS. She received the *2007 – 2008 Volunteer Excellence Award* from ALS Ontario. Donna also volunteered with the Neuromuscular Clinic in Kingston, Ontario as a peer support volunteer. She was a volunteer with Hospice Kingston for two years as part of the Bereavement Support Program.

After being a caregiver to her late husband for six years as he battled ALS and passed away in 2004, Donna made a commitment to be of service to others. For the past sixteen years since her husband's death, she has volunteered in her community, supporting families and caregivers.

Donna has navigated grief, trauma, and loss of self within her personal healing process. Along with her professional expertise, she finds purpose sharing the tools and self-care practices that were instrumental in her healing while creating a new meaningful life.

Donna is now retired from the administrative assistant position she held for thirty-seven years. She enjoys spending time with her children, being a part of her one-year-old grandson's life, and loves being outdoors while tapping into her sense of adventure. Donna continues to offer support to those who find themselves wanting to heal and reconnect with their inner voice—to have meaningful *Conversations with Their Soul.*

www.ingramcontent.com/pod-product-compliance
Lightning Source LLC
Chambersburg PA
CBHW072207100526
44589CB00015B/2407